**THREATS TO
CIVIL LIBERTIES**

Threats to Civil Liberties:
POLICING

Bradley Steffens

**ReferencePoint
Press®**

San Diego, CA

About the Author

Bradley Steffens is a poet, a novelist, and an award-winning author of more than forty nonfiction books for children and young adults. He is a two-time recipient of the San Diego Book Award for Best Young Adult and Children's Nonfiction: his *Giants* won the 2005 award, and his *J.K. Rowling* claimed the 2007 prize. Steffens also received the Theodor S. Geisel Award for best book by a San Diego County author in 2007.

For more information, contact:
ReferencePoint Press, Inc.
PO Box 27779
San Diego, CA 92198
www.ReferencePointPress.com

LIBRARY OF CONGRESS CATALOGING-IN-PUBLICATION DATA

Name: Steffens, Bradley, 1955– author.
Title: Threats to Civil Liberties: Policing/by Bradley Steffens.
Description: San Diego, CA: ReferencePoint Press, Inc., [2019] | Series: Threats to Civil Liberties | Includes bibliographical references and index.
Identifiers: LCCN 2018010453 (print) | LCCN 2018011838 (ebook) | ISBN 9781682824504 (eBook) | ISBN 9781682824498 (hardback)
Subjects: LCSH: Police—United States—Juvenile literature. | Civil rights—United States—Juvenile literature.
Classification: LCC HV8139 (ebook) | LCC HV8139 .S837 2019 (print) | DDC 363.2/30973—dc23
LC record available at https://lccn.loc.gov/2018010453

CONTENTS

The Paradox of Police Power

The founders of the United States believed that every person is born with "with certain unalienable Rights," as Thomas Jefferson put it in the Declaration of Independence. These rights include the rights to "life, liberty and the pursuit of happiness."[1] However, as British philosopher John Locke pointed out eighty-seven years before the Declaration was signed, such rights are not secure. On the contrary, Locke wrote, "the Enjoyment of [a right] is very uncertain, and constantly exposed to the Invasion of others."[2] A person armed with a gun or backed by a gang of hoodlums can deprive other individuals of their individual rights, their property, and even their lives. The way for people to secure their rights is to band together to form a society, ordered by laws. "To secure these rights, Governments are instituted among Men,"[3] Jefferson wrote in the Declaration. But even a government's constitution and laws are not "self-defining and self-enforcing,"[4] as US Supreme Court justice Felix Frankfurter later wrote. Human beings are needed to enforce the laws and secure the rights. Those people are the police. The police make it possible for members of society to enjoy and exercise their rights and freedoms, which

> "The Enjoyment of [a right] is very uncertain, and constantly exposed to the Invasion of others."[2]
>
> —John Locke, a British philosopher and the author of *Two Treatises on Government*

are often referred to as *civil liberties*. But the power of the police can also be used to curtail those civil liberties. This is the paradox of police power.

Necessary Powers

To be effective, the police need power. They not only must be able to detain people who are infringing on the rights of others, but they also must be able to overcome any resistance such people might offer. The police are granted such powers under the law, and they are trained to use their power effectively. If a suspect resists the police physically, the officers may respond with greater physical force or even the use of a nonlethal weapon. If the suspect responds with a weapon, the police can respond with the same or greater force,

> "To secure these rights, Governments are instituted among Men."[3]
>
> —Declaration of Independence

up to and including using deadly force. The concept is simple: If lawbreakers believe they can escape justice by using violence, they will do so. To ensure the safety of the public, maintain the rule of law, and protect individual liberties, the police cannot allow lawbreakers to achieve such an advantage. They are required by the state to maintain order at virtually any cost.

Investing such power in the police is necessary, but it also brings risks. Although the police are more knowledgeable of the law than most people are, and they take an oath to uphold it, they are not perfect. In their zeal to bring criminals to justice, they might use their power in ways that violate the very rights they are sworn to protect.

Limiting the Police

Understanding that police powers can be abused, the founders of the United States added amendments to the Constitution that specifically limit the powers of the police. The Fourth Amendment

A police officer subdues a man during a demonstration. To be effective, the police need power, and are required by law to maintain order at virtually any cost.

protects the public from "unreasonable searches and seizures" by the police and other agents of the government. This amendment specifically mentions "persons, houses, papers, and effects," however, the courts have extended the protection to electronic devices, including telephones, computers, and even cell phones. The Fifth Amendment states that the government, including the police, cannot compel, or force, a person to confess to a crime or serve as a witness against him- or herself. This means that the police cannot torture a person or use extreme mental pressure to make a person talk about a crime. The Sixth Amendment guarantees many things related to trials, including that a person suspected of a crime has the right to have a lawyer present during questioning by the police. Both the Fifth and Fourteenth Amendments state that the government cannot deprive a person "of life, liberty, or property, without due process of law." In other words, all actions by the police must be in accordance with the law and proper legal procedures.

Room for Debate

The wording of these amendments can seem obvious and absolute, but this is not always the case. For example, the Fifth Amendment reads, "No person . . . shall be compelled in any criminal case to be a witness against himself." This seems clear. If a person is on trial, the judge cannot force the defendant to testify. However, what about questions asked by the police before the trial? The courts have ruled that the amendment applies as soon as the police take a person into custody. Does that mean when a person is arrested? Or does it apply to questioning at any time when a person is detained by the police? Torture, threats, and intimidation are not permitted, but what happens when the police are talking among themselves about what might happen to the person in front of them and that person feels a need to speak up about the crime? Has that person been compelled by the police to incriminate him- or herself?

The rules governing police conduct and laws protecting the civil liberties of the public have undergone great changes during the last 250 years. Such rules are affected by the advent of new technologies and by the appearance of threats the founders never envisioned. People do not always agree about where the lines limiting police conduct should be drawn. Some believe the police need greater power in order to safeguard the community. Others believe that police powers need to be further limited to better protect individual rights. Intelligent people on both sides of the argument will continue to debate these issues as long as police are needed to secure the rule of law.

CHAPTER 1

Investigative Procedures

When investigating crimes, the police gather evidence in many ways, including by interviewing witnesses, viewing surveillance footage, examining bank records, conducting forensic analysis, and searching people and their property. The police are limited in some of these procedures by the Fourth Amendment's protections against unreasonable searches and seizures and the Fourteenth Amendment's guarantee of equal protection under the law. Some investigative methods, such as interviewing witnesses, do not conflict with civil liberties. Others, such as searching a suspect's property, do. The requirements for some, such as searching phone records, fall into constitutional gray areas and are still being debated.

Terry Stops

One of the simplest investigative methods is to search a person's outer garments to determine whether the individual is carrying an illegal item or weapon. Such a search is known as a pat down or frisk. Unlike a search of an item a person is carrying, such as a bag, briefcase, or knapsack, a pat down does not require a search warrant, which is a court order that permits a specific search. A police officer only needs a reasonable suspicion that the person presents a danger or is about to engage in a crime. Often that suspicion is triggered by the appearance of something under the clothing that suggests the presence of a weapon, drugs, or other illegal item.

Although frisks are not specifically mentioned in the Constitution, the US Supreme Court ruled that they do not violate its protections. The court addressed the issue in *Terry v. Ohio* (1968), a case in which a plainclothes officer observed three men acting suspiciously. The officer identified himself and questioned the men. Unsatisfied with their answers, the officer patted them down and found that one was carrying a gun. The suspect said the search violated his Fourth Amendment rights, but the Supreme Court ruled that such searches are permitted. The court noted that a frisk is less intrusive than a thorough search after an arrest. It ruled that the interests in crime prevention and in police safety require that the police have some leeway to act before full probable cause has developed. Because of the ruling in *Terry v. Ohio*, pat down searches are now known as Terry stops.

Stop and Frisk

Although individual Terry stops are constitutional, some critics have challenged their constitutionality when they arise not from an individual officer's suspicions but rather from a department-wide program. For example, during the early 2000s the New York City Police Department (NYPD) began to use Terry stops in a large-scale effort to reduce crime. Between January 2004 and June 2012, the police made 4.4 million Terry stops—roughly 600,000 per year—compared to less than 100,000 per year in earlier years. Although the police department said that its officers stopped people because they had reasonable suspicions of potential wrongdoing, the NYPD's own records showed that 88 percent of the stops resulted in no law enforcement action.

This widespread use of these so-called stop-and-frisk searches led the Center for Constitutional Rights to file a federal class action lawsuit against the City of New York. The suit alleged that the NYPD violated the Fourth Amendment through the practice of stopping and frisking without reasonable suspicion. The lawsuit, known as *Floyd et al. v. City of New York et al.*, was heard over nine weeks by US district judge Shira Scheindlin in 2013. On August 12, 2013, Sheindlin ruled that the City of New York

A protester is arrested and searched in front of the White House. The officer is conducting a search known as a pat down, or frisk, which does not require a search warrant.

violated the plaintiffs' rights under the Fourth Amendment's protection against unreasonable search and seizure and the Fourteenth Amendment's guarantee of equal protection under the law. Scheindlin ordered that the NYPD take measures to bring the stop-and-frisk program into compliance with the Constitution. She appointed an independent monitor to oversee stop-and-frisk reforms and report on their progress to the court. She also ordered a pilot program to have officers wear body cameras to record stop-and-frisk activities, believing that the presence of the camera would deter abuses and recordings of the stops would aid in monitoring the activity.

In November 2017, attorney Peter Zimroth, the court-appointed monitor, submitted new stop-and-frisk training materials to the NYPD. The Center for Constitutional Rights considered the action a step forward but not an all-encompassing solution. "Training is not a silver bullet," stated the organization. "Unless and until it is combined with court-ordered reforms to the NYPD's systems for supervising and monitoring stops and disciplining officers who make illegal stops, we are unlikely to see real change in the way the NYPD conducts stops and frisk on the streets of New York City."[5] Without such a change in procedures, critics believe the police department might continue to exceed the power granted to it in the *Terry* decision and violate the civil liberties of law-abiding citizens.

School Drug Sweeps

Since small amounts of drugs are easier to conceal than weapons are, a search for drugs is often more thorough and more intimate than a pat down for weapons. If a person is under arrest, such a careful search is routine. But if the person being searched is not under arrest, this kind of search can raise civil liberties issues.

This was the case at Worth County High School in Sylvester, Georgia, on April 14, 2017. Acting on a tip from some teenagers under arrest that students were selling drugs at the school, Worth County sheriff Jeff Hobby sent a squad of forty deputies to visit the campus and conduct a drug sweep. The officers were looking for twelve students identified by the informants as drug sellers and for any drugs they might have sold to other students. The officers did not have a warrant, but they had the school administration's permission to frisk the students for drugs. During the four-hour lockdown, the school's nine hundred students were ordered into the hallways—girls on one side and boys on the other—and told to stand with their hands on the walls and their legs spread apart. Male officers searched the boys, and female officers searched the girls. Only three of the suspected drug sellers were at school that day, and they did not have any drugs on them. No other drugs were found either. However, after the search nine students complained they were groped during their searches.

Sheriff Hobby and two of the deputies—one male and one female—were indicted by a Worth County grand jury on charges of false imprisonment (for the lengthy lockdown) and violation of their oath of office—both of which were felonies. The charges also included misdemeanor sexual battery. In addition, the students filed a class action lawsuit against the sheriff alleging "unreasonable, aggressive, and invasive" body searches and violations of the Fourth Amendment protection against searches without probable cause. In November 2017, the sheriff's department settled the lawsuit before the case went to trial, agreeing to pay the students $3 million. "This settlement is a victory for the hundreds of Worth County students whose constitutional rights were violated," said Mark Begnaud, an attorney who represented the students. "We hope that this multimillion-dollar settlement will send the message to law enforcement officials everywhere that abuse of power will not be tolerated."[6]

> "This settlement [involving Georgia police officers] is a victory for the hundreds of . . . students whose constitutional rights were violated. We hope that this . . . settlement will send the message to law enforcement officials everywhere that abuse of power will not be tolerated."[6]
>
> —Attorney Mark Begnaud

K-9 Searches

In the Worth County High School case, the sheriff's deputies had a list of suspects but only a vague suspicion that other students

A K-9 police unit provides security at an event in New York. K-9 units are used to conduct searches for suspects, drugs, explosive materials, and other dangerous substances.

might possess drugs. But instead of investigating further and narrowing down the list of possible buyers, the sheriff's department subjected the entire student body to a search. In other school districts, police bring in drug-sniffing dogs to locate possible offenders. In December 2015, for example, Florence-Carlton High School in Ravalli County, Montana, hired a private canine drug detection company to conduct a sweep of the school's parking lot. A drug-sniffing dog signaled an alert on a student's vehicle. A subsequent search found two plastic bags of marijuana and drug paraphernalia. The drugs were turned over to a sheriff's deputy, and the student was given a citation.

Despite the suspicions raised by the K-9 unit at Florence-Carlton High School, Ravalli County district court judge James

Haynes did not allow evidence found by the police and dismissed the case on the grounds that the student's constitutional rights had been violated. Haynes said the search was unlawful because the police did not have particular information that any student had drugs and there was no evidence—and thus no probable cause—that the school had a bad enough problem with drugs to justify a sweeping search with a K-9 unit. The state attorney general's office initially appealed Haynes's ruling but then dismissed the appeal. Instead, it maintained a position that the ruling was not binding outside Ravalli County and that because any school could have a drug problem, K-9 searches would remain a practical means to fight that problem.

The attorney general's office based its position on the findings of the Supreme Court in several decisions involving the use of K-9 units to investigate crimes. In *United States v. Place* (1983), the court ruled that a warrant was not required for a dog to sniff for drugs in a public place, such as an airport, because such an act was not a search under the meaning of the Fourth Amendment. The court noted that the only purpose of the dog's sniff is to locate illegal drugs. This is different from a police officer's search of a bag or suitcase, which might not only turn up drugs but also evidence of other criminal activity. Because a dog's sniff can detect only one thing—the presence of drugs—it is considered a limited test. Such a limited test can be allowed under the amendment, the court said. Similarly, in *Illinois v. Caballes* (2005), the court found that allowing a dog to sniff a vehicle for drugs during a routine traffic stop was constitutional. However, the court emphasized that such a search must be quick. A prolonged search without probable cause would be unreasonable, the court said, and would violate the motorist's constitutional rights.

Searches of the Home

The Supreme Court has placed limits on the free use of drug-sniffing dogs, however. That limit is at the home and its immediate surroundings. In *Florida v. Jardines* (2013), the high court ruled that an alert produced by a drug-sniffing dog at the front door of a home qualifies as a search under the Fourth Amendment and therefore requires a warrant to conduct. "When it comes to the Fourth Amendment, the home is first among equals," wrote Justice Antonin Scalia for the majority. "At the Amendment's 'very core' stands 'the right of a man to retreat into his own home and there be free from unreasonable governmental intrusion.' This right would be of little practical value if the State's agents could stand in a home's porch or side garden and trawl for evidence with impunity." [7]

It is also a violation of a person's civil liberties when the police intrude into the home using high-tech devices. In 1991 federal agents in Florence, Oregon, suspected that Danny Lee Kyllo was growing marijuana in his home. The agents scanned Kyllo's home with a thermal imaging device to see whether the amount of heat emanating from it suggested the presence of high-intensity lamps used for growing marijuana indoors. The scan revealed that Kyllo's garage was hotter than the rest of his house and warmer than the other units in the triplex where he lived. The police presented the thermal imaging findings and other information to a federal judge. The judge issued a warrant to search Kyllo's home, and the agents found marijuana growing. Kyllo was indicted on a federal drug charge.

His attorneys tried to suppress the evidence gathered from the search, arguing that the thermal scan violated Kyllo's civil liberties under the Fourth Amendment. The federal judge hearing the case did not agree, but the Supreme Court did. "Where . . . the Government uses a device that is not in general public use, to explore details of the home that would previously have been unknowable without physical intrusion, the surveillance is a 'search'

> "At the [Fourth] Amendment's 'very core' stands 'the right of a man to retreat into his own home and there be free from unreasonable governmental intrusion.'" [7]
>
> —Justice Antonin Scalia of the US Supreme Court

Thermal Imaging Does Not Invade the Home

John Paul Stevens was a US Supreme Court justice until he retired in 2010. In this excerpt from his dissent in *Kyllo v. United States*, he argues that detecting warmth from outside a home does not violate the Fourth Amendment's protection against unreasonable searches.

> There is, in my judgment, a distinction of constitutional magnitude between "through-the-wall surveillance" that gives the observer or listener direct access to information in a private area, on the one hand, and the thought processes used to draw inferences from information in the public domain, on the other hand. The Court has crafted a rule that purports to deal with direct observations of the inside of the home, but the case before us merely involves indirect deductions from "off-the-wall" surveillance, that is, observations of the exterior of the home. Those observations were made with a fairly primitive thermal imager that gathered data exposed on the outside of petitioner's home but did not invade any constitutionally protected interest in privacy.

Quoted in Justia, "Kyllo v. United States, 533 U.S. 27 (2001)." https://supreme.justia.com.

and is presumptively unreasonable without a warrant,"[8] wrote Justice Scalia for the majority in *Kyllo v. United States* (2001).

Tracking a Vehicle

In *Jardines* and *Kyllo*, the Supreme Court held that the police had intruded into the home of a person under investigation without a warrant. What happens, however, when people leave their homes? Do they lose their Fourth Amendment protections? Are there any limits to what the police can do then? This was the issue in a case known as *United States v. Jones* (2012). In 2005 FBI agents attached a GPS tracking device on the undercarriage of a

Thermal Imaging Invades Privacy

Justice Antonin Scalia wrote the Supreme Court's majority opinion in *Kyllo v. United States*. Scalia held that thermal imaging invades the privacy of the home and violates the Fourth Amendment. Following is an excerpt of that opinion.

> In the case of the search of the interior of homes . . . there is a ready criterion, with roots deep in the common law, of the minimal expectation of privacy that exists. . . . To withdraw protection of this minimum expectation would be to permit police technology to erode the privacy guaranteed by the Fourth Amendment. We think that obtaining by sense-enhancing technology any information regarding the interior of the home that could not otherwise have been obtained without physical "intrusion into a constitutionally protected area" constitutes a search at least where (as here) the technology in question is not in general public use. This assures preservation of that degree of privacy against government that existed when the Fourth Amendment was adopted.

Quoted in Justia, "Kyllo v. United States, 533 U.S. 27 (2001)." https://supreme.justia.com.

Jeep Grand Cherokee registered to the wife of a suspected drug dealer named Antoine Jones. Although the agents had obtained a search warrant, the warrant had expired before the device was attached to the vehicle. The agents tracked the movements of the vehicle for twenty-eight days.

Jones's attorneys sought to suppress the GPS location data on the basis that it qualified as a search under the Fourth Amendment and, therefore, required a warrant. The court allowed the evidence to be presented, and it was used to connect Jones to a house that contained $850,000 in cash and nearly 220 pounds (100 kg) of cocaine. The jury found Jones guilty, and the district court sentenced him to life imprisonment. Jones's attorneys appealed the case to the Supreme Court. The high court found that Jones's civil liberties had been violated, ruling that the Fourth Amendment's protections extend not only to a person but also to a person's possessions, or effects, outside the home. "It is beyond dispute that a vehicle is an 'effect' as that term is used in the [Fourth] Amendment," wrote Justice Scalia for the majority in *United States v. Jones*. "We hold that the Government's installation of a GPS device on a target's vehicle, and its use of that device to monitor the vehicle's movements, constitutes a 'search.'"[9]

Like *Jardines* and *Kyllo*, *Jones* involved police trespassing on the personal property of a suspect. However, the court had decided in another case that a person's protection against searches extends beyond the home and property to any place where the person has a reasonable expectation of privacy. That case is *Katz v. United States* (1967).

Protecting People, Not Places

In 1965 the FBI began to suspect that Charles Katz, a well-known predictor of the outcomes of basketball games, known as a basketball handicapper, was placing bets on basketball games from Los Angeles, where he lived, with betting parlors in other states. Interstate gambling outside of a licensed facility, such as a casino, is a violation of federal law, so Katz placed his bets from public telephone booths to avoid detection by law enforcement officials. The FBI placed listening devices on the exteriors of the two phone booths Katz used the most and recorded him making bets.

Katz's attorneys argued that the FBI's surveillance of the phone booths violated Katz's civil liberties. In an earlier case, *Olmstead v. United States* (1928), the Supreme Court had ruled that police could listen in on a person's telephone conversations by tapping into lines located outside the home. The court reasoned that wiretapping was permissible because the police were not trespassing on the person's property to do it. However, in *Katz*, the court reversed itself. "The Fourth Amendment protects people, not places," wrote Justice Potter Stewart for the majority. "What a person knowingly exposes to the public, even in his own home or office, is not a subject of Fourth Amendment protection. But what he seeks to preserve as private, even in an area accessible to the public, may be constitutionally protected."[10] The court held that when Katz closed the door to the telephone booth, he expected his conversation to be private. It was a reasonable expectation, the court explained, because others in society would recognize his desire for privacy. The court held that the government needed a search warrant to intrude on Katz's privacy.

Using the reasonable expectation of privacy standard, the courts have ruled that the police must have a warrant to listen in on phone conversations wherever they take place (except on

> "The Fourth Amendment protects people, not places. What a person . . . seeks to preserve as private, even in an area accessible to the public, may be constitutionally protected."[10]
>
> —Justice Potter Stewart of the US Supreme Court

Cell phones regularly send out GPS signals to cell towers. There has been debate about whether this information can be used as evidence under the third-party doctrine.

a crowded airplane or other public venue where they can be clearly overheard by witnesses). Conversely, the court has ruled that the police do not need a warrant when no reasonable expectation of privacy exists. For example, in *Smith v. Maryland* (1979), the court held that a record of telephone numbers dialed by a person is not protected by the Fourth Amendment. "All telephone users realize that they must 'convey' phone numbers to the telephone company, since it is through telephone company switching equipment that their calls are completed," wrote Justice Harry Blackmun for the majority in *Smith*. "We doubt that people in general entertain any actual expectation of privacy in the numbers they dial."[11]

The Third-Party Doctrine

The idea that people give up their Fourth Amendment protections when they willingly give information to a company is known as the third-party doctrine. This doctrine was established in a case known as *United States v. Miller* (1976). In this case, agents from the Treasury Department's Bureau of Alcohol, Tobacco, and Firearms (ATF) obtained grand jury subpoenas and presented them to the bank where a bootlegging suspect, Mitch Miller, had an account. The subpoenas asked for the bank to turn over all of Miller's financial records. The bank complied, and Miller was charged with various crimes related to operating an unlicensed distillery. He was convicted, but he appealed on the grounds that the ATF had violated his Fourth Amendment protections by failing to obtain a search warrant. The Supreme Court ruled that business records given to a third party are not protected by the Fourth Amendment, so no search warrant was required. "All of the documents obtained, including financial statements and deposit slips, contain only information voluntarily conveyed to the banks and exposed to their employees in the ordinary course of business," wrote Justice Lewis Powell for the majority. "This Court has held repeatedly that the Fourth Amendment does not prohibit the obtaining of information revealed to a third party and conveyed by him to Government authorities."[12] Since then, the third-party doctrine has been applied to bank or credit card company records, details of Internet searches conducted through a search engine such as Google or Bing, and even e-mails left on a third-party server for long periods of time.

A 2018 case heard by the Supreme Court, *Carpenter v. United States*, raised issues about the limits of the third-party doctrine. The man bringing the case, Timothy Ivory Carpenter, was sentenced to 116 years in prison for his part in a series of armed robberies at Radio Shacks and T-Mobile stores in Michigan and Ohio in 2011. At his trial, the prosecutors presented evidence that he was in the vicinity of the stores at the times of the robberies. This evidence was based on cell phone records obtained by the police without a warrant. There is no question that the records of cell phone calls, which were kept by the cell phone service provider for billing and other purposes, are covered by the third-party doctrine. However, cell phones send signals to cell phone towers not only when a person dials a call but also when cell phone apps automatically contact computers on the Internet for various purposes. Carpenter's attorneys argued that when apps automatically feed location information to the cell phone provider, the person is not freely conveying the information as they do when making a call. These automatic signals, the lawyers argued, should not be considered as third-party information.

Michael R. Dreeben, the attorney representing the government, disagreed. "The technology here is new, but the legal principles that this Court has articulated under the Fourth Amendment are not," Dreeben argued. "The cell phone companies in this case function essentially as witnesses being asked to produce business records of their own transactions with customers."[13] Speaking from the bench, Justice Elena Kagan appeared to disagree. She asked Dreeben how Carpenter's case was different from *Jones*, the GPS case. She read from Justice Samuel Alito's concurring opinion in *Jones*: "'Society's expectation has been that law enforcement and others would not, and indeed in the main simply cannot, monitor and catalogue every single movement of an individual's'—there it was a car—'for a long period.' So how is it different from that?" Dreeben replied that *Jones* involved attaching the GPS tracking device to a vehicle, which trespassed on the suspect's property. "Now, you're exactly right, there were different means," said Kagan, "but in both cases, you have a new technology that allows for 24/7 tracking and a conclusion by a number of justices in *Jones* that that was an altogether new and different thing that did intrude on people's expectations of who would be watching them when."[14]

As technology evolves, allowing for even closer surveillance of individuals, the courts will have to continue to decide what information the police can obtain without a warrant and what is protected by the Fourth Amendment.

CHAPTER 2

Interrogation Techniques

Once an arrest has been made, the police attempt to learn everything possible about the crime by interrogating, or questioning, the accused. "Questioning is an indispensable instrumentality of justice,"[15] wrote Justice Robert H. Jackson in 1944. Police might ask about whereabouts of evidence, such as weapons, drugs, or stolen items. They might ask whether anyone was hurt in the commission of the crime. They also will try to learn if the arrestee was working alone or had accomplices.

The techniques employed by the police during the interrogation of suspects can raise civil liberties issues because the people in custody have rights that are protected by the Fourth, Fifth, and Sixth Amendments. Police officers who violate these constitutional limits threaten civil liberties and jeopardize the cases they are trying to build, as the evidence they obtain may not be allowed at trial or on appeal.

> **"Questioning is an indispensable instrumentality of justice."[15]**
>
> —Justice Robert H. Jackson of the US Supreme Court

Once a person is under arrest, the police have the power—granted by state and federal government—to search the clothing and body of the accused for weapons, which could be used against them, or for evidence of a crime. "The Fourth Amendment has never been held to require that every valid search and seizure be effected under the authority of a search warrant," wrote Chief Justice Fred M. Vinson in *Harris v. United States* (1947). "Search and seizure incident to lawful arrest is a practice of ancient origin, and has long been

The police have the right to search a suspect's body for evidence of a struggle, such as cuts and scratches. However, there are limits to the search of persons and their possessions without a warrant.

an integral part of the law enforcement."[16] If they have reasonable suspicion, police officers can check the contents of a wallet or purse, looking for drugs, stolen credit cards, false identification, or anything else that might help convict the accused of wrongdoing. They can examine clothing for blood spatter, the residue of gunshots, or microscopic evidence, such as hairs, pollen, and fibers. They can check for the presence of drugs or alcohol in the arrestee's system. They can even examine the person's body for evidence of a struggle, such as cuts, scratches, bite marks, or tissue beneath the fingernails. Nevertheless, there are limits to the search of a person and their possessions. For example, in a case known as *Riley v. California* (2014), the Supreme Court said that an arrestee's cell phone could not be searched without a warrant.

Portable Minicomputers

In *Riley*, police had searched the contents of a cell phone belonging to a man who had been arrested on weapons charges. The police had proceeded on the belief that they were allowed to search through the cell phone just as they might search through the pockets, wallet, or bag of a person arrested for a crime. The high court disagreed, however. "Cell phones differ in both a quantitative and a qualitative sense from other objects that might be kept on an arrestee's person," wrote Chief Justice John Roberts for a unanimous court in *Riley*. "The term 'cell phone' is itself misleading shorthand; many of these devices are in fact minicomputers that also happen to have the capacity to be used as a telephone." He continued,

> One of the most notable distinguishing features of modern cell phones is their immense storage capacity. Before cell phones, a search of a person was limited by physical realities and tended as a general matter to constitute only a narrow intrusion on privacy. Most people cannot lug around every piece of mail they have received for the past several months, every picture they have taken, or every book or article they have read—nor would they have any reason to attempt to do so. . . .
>
> In 1926, [Judge] Learned Hand observed that it is 'a totally different thing to search a man's pockets and use against him what they contain, from ransacking his house for everything which may incriminate him.' If his pockets contain a cell phone, however, that is no longer true. Indeed, a cell phone search would typically expose to the government far more than the most exhaustive search of a house: A phone not only contains in digital form many sensitive records previously found in the home; it also contains a broad array of private information never found in a home in any form—unless the phone is.[17]

In *Riley*, the court ruled that cell phones can be searched, but a search warrant is required. "Modern cell phones are not just another technological convenience," stated the court.

> With all they contain and all they may reveal, they hold for many Americans "the privacies of life." The fact that technology now allows an individual to carry such information

in his hand does not make the information any less worthy of the protection for which the Founders fought. Our answer to the question of what police must do before searching a cell phone seized incident to an arrest is accordingly simple—get a warrant.[18]

Even though a person is under arrest, the police still need a warrant to search not only the arrestee's cell phone but also his or her home, vehicles, or other property. The only exceptions are when the police have reason to believe a person's life may be in danger or that evidence will be destroyed if they must wait for a warrant.

Conning the Suspect

The police have wide latitude in their questioning of those in custody. For example, they are not required to tell the truth during questioning. They can mislead the person with any number of guises. For example, they can claim that an accomplice has confessed to a crime and is providing information against the person being questioned, even if that is not the case. Similarly, the police can claim that they have found physical evidence linking the person to a crime, even though that might not be true. These ruses are designed to convince the accused that they are in a hopeless situation and that things will be better for them if they confess. As one police officer put it, "Interrogation is not a matter of forcing suspects to confess but of 'conning' them."[19]

> "Modern cell phones are not just another technological convenience. With all they contain and all they may reveal, they hold for many Americans 'the privacies of life.'"[18]
>
> —Chief Justice of the United States John Roberts

However, feeding suspects misinformation can violate their civil liberties if it creates extreme mental pressure and compels, or coerces, them into saying things that suggest their own guilt. For example, police in Escondido, California, questioned fourteen-year-old

Michael Crowe several times about the murder of his twelve-year-old sister, Stephanie, including conducting a six-hour session. Crowe did not ask for an attorney or his parents to be present. Crowe denied killing his sister over and over, but the police kept feeding him lies. For example, they told him they had found Stephanie's blood in his room and his hair in Stephanie's hand, but they had not. When they asked him what he did with the murder weapon, he said, "Why? God. No. I don't know. I didn't do it. I'll swear to that." When they told him he had failed a lie detector test, he said, "I don't know why it says that. I told the truth on every question." Under the weight of police insistence that they had evidence linking him to the crime, Crowe broke down. "Why are you doing this to me?" he asked the police. "I didn't do this to her. I couldn't. God. Why? I can't even believe myself anymore. I don't know if I did it or not. I didn't, though." Finally, Crowe confessed to killing his sister, even though he could not remember doing it. "Like I said, the only way I even know I did this is that she's dead and that the evidence says I did it."[20] Months later, Judge John Thompson threw out Michael Crowe's confession as illegally obtained. Charges against Crowe were dropped when another person was arrested for Stephanie's murder.

Crowe's forced confession was not unique. The National Registry of Exonerations, which tracks cases in which convictions are overturned, often because of DNA evidence, has found that 227 of the 1,810 exonerations in the United States between 1989 and 2016 were of innocent men and women who had confessed. "That number may be much higher than we report," states the registry. "The only false convictions that we can count are those that result in exoneration."[21] Of course, false confessions are more common in longer interrogations. As a result, 70 percent of exonerations with false confessions are murder cases.

Self-Incrimination

The Fifth Amendment was derived from a seventeenth-century British law that banned the practices of torture and forced confessions. Under the Fifth Amendment standard, a person cannot be forced by torture, threats, intimidation, or coercion to give information about a crime that could be used as evidence against him or her. As a result, the government must prove its cases with its own evidence without depending on statements of the defendants. In trials, juries are instructed not to interpret a defendant's or witness's refusal to answer questions to be an admission of guilt. A person's use of this protection is sometimes known as pleading the Fifth.

The Fifth Amendment does not prevent accused people from talking to the police or even confessing their guilt, if they wish to do so. However, such suspects must waive their rights knowingly, intelligently, and voluntarily. To decide whether such a waiver has been made, a court must consider all of the events surrounding it to ensure that the suspect freely decided to give up the right to silence.

> "The person in custody must, prior to interrogation, be clearly informed that he has the right to remain silent, and that anything he says will be used against him in court."[22]
>
> —Chief Justice of the United States Earl Warren

The Miranda Rule

The Fifth Amendment applies to not only what is said in court but also to any statement made after the police have taken a suspect into custody. To ensure that the Fifth Amendment rights of the accused are fully in force as soon as the person is in custody, the Supreme Court laid out specific procedures for the police to follow. In a case known as *Miranda v. Arizona* (1966), the court declared,

> The person in custody must, prior to interrogation, be clearly informed that he has the right to remain silent, and that anything he says will be used against him in court; he must be clearly informed that he has the right to consult with a lawyer and to have the lawyer with him during inter-

rogation, and that, if he is indigent [i.e., too poor to afford counsel], a lawyer will be appointed to represent him.[22]

This ruling led to the now-familiar Mirandizing of suspects that has been featured in countless crime dramas. These procedures were viewed by some in law enforcement as burdensome. However, advising the accused of their rights has proved to be a positive development for law enforcement. It has meant that anything suspects say after being advised of their rights can and most likely will be used at trial.

Although the Miranda rule is clear, its implementation sometimes raises civil liberties issues. For example, English is not the first language spoken by many people in the United States, and

The police have wide latitude in their questioning of those in custody. In pursuit of a confession, police might mislead suspects or misconstrue evidence linking them to a crime.

many do not speak it at all. The attorneys for suspects who speak foreign languages, including Spanish, Arabic, Korean, and Somali, have succeeded in having some confessions thrown out of court because the suspects received their Miranda warning in English. Other suspects have had statements kept out of trial because the translations given were not accurate and the suspects did not fully understand what they were being told. In one case, *Garner v. Mitchell* (2007), the US Court of Appeals for the Sixth Circuit reversed the conviction and death sentence of a man with a very low IQ, finding that the defendant did not knowingly and intelligently give up his Miranda rights.

Manipulating the Suspect

If a person taken into police custody invokes his/her Miranda rights and refuses to talk, police cannot then intentionally manipulate or pressure individuals to talk. For example, on January 17, 1975, Thomas Innis was arrested for the robbery and shotgun murder of a taxicab driver near a school for handicapped children in Providence, Rhode Island. Innis was advised of his Miranda rights by the arresting officer and then advised again by a police sergeant and a captain who arrived at the scene a few minutes later. After the last Miranda warnings, Innis said he wanted to speak with an attorney.

Because Innis invoked his Fifth Amendment rights, the captain ordered the three officers transporting Innis to police headquarters not to question the suspect. The officers followed the order, but as they drove along, they talked to each other about the case, including the fact that the murder weapon—a sawed-off shotgun—had not been found. One of the officers, Joseph Gleckman, said, "I frequent this area while on patrol and there's a lot of handicapped children running around this area, and God forbid one of them might hurt themselves."[23] Another officer, Richard McKenna, agreed, stating, "We should, you know, continue to search for the weapon and try to find it."[24] The third officer, Walter Williams, did not participate in the conversation, but he later testified, "[Gleckman] said it would be too bad if the little girl—I believe he said little girl—would pick up the gun, maybe kill herself."[25] At that point, Innis spoke up, telling the officers that he would show them where the shotgun was hidden. The officers advised Innis of his rights again, but he led them to the location of the shotgun. His statements regarding the location of the weapon were used against him at trial, and he was found guilty.

Innis's attorney argued that the police held the conversation to manipulate Innis into talking. The Rhode Island Supreme Court agreed, stating that the police had subjected Innis to "subtle compulsion,"[26] which was the equivalent of interrogation and therefore a violation of his Fifth Amendment rights. The US Supreme Court reviewed the case and overturned the Rhode Island court's decision. The high court agreed with the Rhode Island court that there are ways of obtaining information from suspects other than direct questioning. The court held that the Miranda safeguards apply when a suspect is subjected not only to "express questioning" but also to "its functional equivalent." The court defined the functional equivalent of interrogation as "words or actions on the part of police officers that they *should have known* were reasonably likely to elicit an incriminating response."[27]

In the case of Innis, the court also agreed with the Rhode Island court that "it may be said that respondent was subjected to 'subtle compulsion.'" However, the high court added that "it must also be established that a suspect's incriminating response was the product of words or actions on the part of the police that they should have known were reasonably likely to elicit an incriminating response, which was not established here."[28] The court did not believe the police officers were intending to influence Innis, so it ruled that his statements could be used against him. As a result, the court let Innis's conviction stand.

When Silence Is Not Enough

According to the *Miranda* ruling, the police must advise a person in custody of the right to remain silent, but what happens

Silence Does Not Invoke the Fifth Amendment

Law professor Albert W. Alschuler states that merely falling silent does not necessarily indicate that a person is invoking the Fifth Amendment, as the dissenters in *Salinas v. Texas* maintain.

> The Salinas dissenters said that, when asked about the shotgun and shells, the suspect "fell silent." People can confess, however, by using gestures or American Sign Language, and looking to the floor, biting one's lip, and refusing to answer can look a lot like a confession too. Under some circumstances, suddenly falling silent can communicate much the same message as the statement, "I'm sunk." Especially when a refusal to answer is accompanied by a revealing change in facial expression or body language or by a sigh or a groan, no basis for drawing a line between silence and speech is apparent. Why draw it?...
>
> Admitting incriminating statements while excluding incriminating silence does not remain neutral between silence and speech. It does not merely afford suspects "a free choice to admit, to deny, or to refuse to answer." It treats suspects who remain silent more favorably than suspects who speak. Only a glorification of noncooperation with the government can explain this tilt, and glorifying noncooperation with a justified governmental inquiry is backwards.

Albert W. Alschuler, "Miranda's Fourfold Failure," *Public Law and Legal Theory Working Papers*, Chicago Unbound, University of Chicago Law School, 2017. https://chicagounbound.uchicago.edu.

when a person is not being held against his or her will? Can the person's statements be used as evidence? What if the person refuses to answer but does not specifically claim his or her Fifth Amendment right to silence? In 2013 the Supreme Court said such statements—and even a person's silence—could be used in court.

In January 1993, Houston police began to suspect that Genovevo Salinas had murdered two brothers the previous month. They asked Salinas to come to the police station to take photographs and to clear him as a suspect. At the station, police took Salinas into what he described as an interview room. Because he was free to leave at any time, the police did not give Salinas a Miranda warning. The police asked Salinas questions about the murder of the brothers. He answered until the police asked him whether shells from his own shotgun would match those found at the murder scene. At that point Salinas refused to answer. He did

Silence Invokes the Fifth Amendment

Justice Stephen G. Breyer wrote a dissenting opinion to the Supreme Court's decision in *Salinas v. Texas*. In this excerpt, he argues that refusing to answer an incriminating question automatically invokes the Fifth Amendment.

It is consequently not surprising that this Court, more than half a century ago, explained that "no ritualistic formula is necessary in order to invoke the [Fifth Amendment] privilege." Thus, a prosecutor may not comment on a defendant's failure to testify at trial—even if neither the defendant nor anyone else ever mentions a Fifth Amendment right not to do so. Circumstances, not a defendant's statement, tie the defendant's silence to the right. Similarly, a prosecutor may not comment on the fact that a defendant in custody, after receiving Miranda warnings, "stood mute"—regardless of whether he "claimed his privilege" in so many words. Again, it is not any explicit statement but, instead, the defendant's deeds (silence) and circumstances (receipt of the warnings) that tie together silence and constitutional right. Most lower courts have so construed the law, even where the defendant, having received Miranda warnings, answers some questions while remaining silent as to others.

Quoted in Justia, "Salinas v. Texas, 570 U.S. ___ (2013)." https://supreme.justia.com.

not say anything about using his Fifth Amendment rights. At his trial, the prosecutor used his silence against him and convinced the jury of his guilt. Salinas was found guilty of murder and sentenced to twenty years in prison.

Salinas's attorneys argued to the Supreme Court that by remaining silent, Salinas was invoking his Fifth Amendment protection against self-incrimination. In a 5–4 decision, the Supreme Court disagreed. The court ruled that Salinas's refusal to answer was not protected by the Fifth Amendment because Salinas never stated that he was exercising his right. "Petitioner's Fifth Amendment claim fails because he did not expressly invoke the privilege against self-incrimination in response to the officer's

When a person is arrested, the police must inform them of their Fifth Amendment rights. This is known as the Miranda Law. Suspects are told that they have the right to remain silent and to have an attorney present during questioning.

question," wrote Justice Samuel Alito for the majority in *Salinas v. Texas* (2013). Quoting from *Minnesota v. Murphy* (1984) and *United States v. Monia* (1943), Alito continued, "It has long been settled that the privilege 'generally is not self-executing' and that a witness who desires its protection 'must claim it.'"[29]

The four dissenting justices strongly disagreed. "The Fifth Amendment prohibits prosecutors from commenting on an individual's silence where that silence amounts to an effort to avoid becoming 'a witness against himself,'"[30] wrote Justice Stephen G. Breyer for the dissenters. For support, Breyer pointed to the Supreme Court's ruling in *Griffin v. California* (1965), which stated that a comment by a prosecuting attorney about a defendant's failure to testify is a violation of the Fifth Amendment. Breyer and the other dissenters thought the same rule should apply to a suspect's silence before trial. Breyer pointed out that in *Miranda* itself, the court found that "an individual, when silent, need not expressly invoke the Fifth Amendment if there are 'inherently compelling pressures' not to do so."[31] The pressures Salinas faced when questioned about the shotgun shells created such pressures, Breyer wrote, because Salinas knew that if he answered he would be incriminating himself. Civil libertarians and other commentators criticized the court's ruling. "It all seems ridiculously terrifying, this idea that in order to claim your Fifth Amendment, you now need to know how to call the on-the-fly legal equivalent of 'safesies,'"[32] wrote Alexander Abad-Santos for the *Atlantic*.

> "It all seems ridiculously terrifying, this idea that in order to claim your Fifth Amendment, you now need to know how to call the on-the-fly legal equivalent of 'safesies.'"[32]
>
> —Reporter Alexander Abad-Santos

An Exception for Public Safety

In rare cases, the police can question suspects about weapons without Mirandizing if they believe the public is in danger. If the questioning reveals the location of a weapon, the information can be used at trial, even though no Miranda warning was given. This is known as the public safety exception to the Fifth Amendment. This exception arose during the case of Benjamin Quarles, who was arrested for rape in 1980. After midnight on September 11, 1980, a woman stopped police officers outside an A&P supermarket in Queens, New York, and told them she had been raped by a man who was in the store with a gun. The officers located a man who fit the description. The suspect ran but was caught. One of the officers frisked Quarles and found an empty gun holster. When asked where the gun was, Quarles told the officers where they would find it. Quarles's attorneys later said his statement could not be used against him because the police had not advised him of his rights before asking him about the weapon. The Supreme Court disagreed. "Overriding considerations of public safety justify the officer's failure to provide Miranda warnings before he asked questions devoted to locating the abandoned weapon," wrote Chief Justice William Rehnquist for the majority. "We conclude that the need for answers to questions in a situation posing a threat to public safety outweighs the need for the . . . rule protecting the . . . privilege against self-incrimination."[33]

As the high court's ruling in the *Quarles* case shows, although individual civil liberties are important, they do not always outweigh other competing values and interests. The police are responsible for maintaining public safety and protecting innocent lives. They must be allowed to do this within reason, without jeopardizing the cases against the criminals they are trying to bring to justice.

CHAPTER 3

The Use of Force

Police officers are authorized to use force—up to and including deadly force—to protect the safety of their community, their fellow officers, and themselves. People apprehended by police must comply with police orders. If they forcibly resist, the police can and will use force against them. Although police departments provide guidelines for the use of force and training in its use, individual officers typically make the final decision about when to employ force and how much to use. Because using force is ultimately an individual decision, officers occasionally are accused of using more force than necessary to resolve a situation. This excessive use of force can violate the civil liberties of suspects and arrestees.

The Use-of-Force Continuum

In the course of their duties, the police sometimes come in contact with people who resist arrest. In such cases, the police will use whatever force is necessary to subdue the person. This can include using a Taser, baton, or even a gun. In extreme cases, SWAT teams deploy military-grade weaponry. Any time a weapon is deployed, there is a danger that the officer will use more force than is necessary.

Police officers are trained to exercise force in accordance with what is known as the use-of-force continuum. This training model provides law enforcement officers with guidelines as to how much force may be used against a resisting person in a given situation. Typically, the use-of-force continuum consists of five steps that escalate depending on the amount of resistance the officer encounters. The five steps, in escalating order, include officer presence, verbal communication, empty-hand control, inter-mediate weapons, and lethal force. Usually the mere presence of an officer is enough to gain control of a situation (officer presence). If a person ignores the officer's presence, the officer might issue nonthreatening requests, such as "may I see your driver's license," or direct commands aimed at gaining compliance, such as "stop" or "don't move" (verbal communication). If the person fails to com-ply, the officer may use bodily force to gain control of a situation (empty-hand control). This can include a soft technique, in which an officer uses holds and joint locks to restrain an individual, or hard techniques, such as punches and kicks. If the person fights back, the police officer may employ nonlethal chemical, electronic, or im-pact weapons on a subject (intermediate weapons). This includes pepper spray; conducted energy devices, such as a Taser, which discharges a high-voltage jolt of electricity at a distance; or a baton for striking a person. If the person confronts the officer with a knife or a gun, the officer will use a service revolver or another weapon likely to cause permanent injury or death to a subject (lethal force). Lethal force may only be used when a suspect poses a serious threat to the officer or another individual.

The Taser Controversy

The continuum of force is designed to protect the safety of the officer and the rights of the person confronted by the officer, in-cluding the right to life. However, the officer may have only sec-onds to move from one level to the next. In a rapidly escalating situation, the officers sometimes exceed what is required to gain control. This is known as excessive force. For example, Tasers are employed as nonlethal force when officers' lives or the lives of others are not in immediate danger. However, the Reuters news service examined thousands of court records, police reports, and news stories from 1983 through July 2017. It found that 1,005

A police officer demonstrates the use of a Taser stun gun. The Taser can be employed by an officer as a nonlethal attempt to gain control of someone who is resisting arrest.

people have died in the United States following police use of Tasers. When the police kill a civilian who does not present a threat that requires deadly force, the death is often considered a case of excessive force. More than four hundred wrongful death lawsuits have been filed against police and the municipalities in which suspects died after being shocked with a Taser.

Choke Holds

People have died from nonlethal empty-hand control as well, especially choke holds and strangleholds. In a choke hold, an officer places one arm across a person's throat and uses the other arm to lock the hold in place, constricting the suspect's breathing and rendering him or her compliant. In a stranglehold, the officer uses a bent arm to put pressure on the sides of a suspect's neck to reduce or prevent blood from reaching the brain, rendering the subject unconscious.

In a highly publicized 2014 case, a medical examiner ruled that a police officer's choke hold caused the death of Eric Garner, who was under arrest for selling so-called loosies, which are untaxed, loose cigarettes. Officer Daniel Pantaleo first tried to restrain Garner by putting Garner's wrist behind his back. When Garner pulled away, Pantaleo placed his arm around Garner's neck and wrestled him to the ground. Pantaleo released Garner after about fifteen seconds, but other officers held Garner face-down on the sidewalk for several minutes. The medical examiner found that the cause of Garner's death was compression of the neck from a choke hold and compression of the chest while the police held him face-down on the sidewalk. Garner's death was ruled a homicide, meaning that it was caused by intentional actions, but it was not necessarily an intentional or criminal death.

Because the officer's actions were found to be unintentional, a grand jury declined to indict Pantaleo on criminal charges, sparking demonstrations worldwide. Demonstrators chanted, "I can't breathe," the words Garner uttered eleven times during the incident, to protest the fact that Pantaleo was not held responsible for Garner's death. The US Justice Department launched an investigation into possible civil rights violations during the incident. The City of New York settled a lawsuit filed by Garner's family, paying a $5.9 million settlement. Pantaleo was stripped of his badge and gun and was removed from street duties during the investigation and is awaiting the outcome of the federal investigation.

In 2017 Las Vegas Metropolitan Police Department (LVMPD) officer Kenneth Lopera was charged with involuntary manslaughter in the death of a carjacking suspect named Tashii Farmer Brown after administering a stranglehold that rendered Brown unconscious. Lopera and his partner had already used a Taser on Brown several times without managing to subdue him. Lopera then used the lateral vascular neck restraint (LVNR) technique to subdue Brown. An LVNR compresses the carotid arteries in the neck to render the subject unconscious within seconds without obstructing the person's airway. After handcuffing the suspect, Lopera and his partner noticed that Brown was not breathing. They called medical personnel and performed CPR until paramedics arrived. Brown died an hour later at the hospital.

"The incident of a man dying in police custody today is one more reason why the use of choke-hold practices must stop," said Tod Story, the executive director of the Nevada chapter of the American Civil Liberties Union (ACLU). "Too many people have died as a result of this type of excessive force and too many questions remain about the use of choke-holds by our police."[34] In the wake of Brown's death, the LVMPD reclassified the LVNR as deadly force, only to be used in response to an intent to harm an individual or officer. "It is unfortunate that it took the death of Tashii Farmer Brown . . . for the department to take this action," said Story. "This dangerous, potentially deadly technique should not be utilized subjectively by officers, and is now appropriately classified as deadly force and only to be utilized in response to situations in which suspects have intent to harm."[35]

> "The incident of a man dying in police custody today is one more reason why the use of choke-hold practices must stop."[34]
>
> —Attorney Tod Story of the ACLU

Deadly Force

If nonlethal methods fail to stop aggressive suspects, the police resort to lethal force, often with deadly consequences. Police officers are trained to stop aggressors, not to try to shoot guns out of their hands or wound them, as is sometimes depicted in movies and television. In recent years, police have killed nearly one thousand people each year in the United States. In a country with more than 2.7 million deaths per year from all causes, deaths from police shootings are rare; fewer than one out of every 2,700 deaths are from police shootings. There are more than 750,000 police officers in the United States, and very few are ever involved in a shooting. "The average number of OIS [officer-involved shootings] for an officer over the course of an entire career is literally close to zero,"[36] said Mark Iris, a lecturer at Northwestern University and a former head of Chicago's police review board. Nevertheless, in every use of lethal force, the state deprives a person of his or her most basic right—the right to life—without which no other rights can be enjoyed. As a result, every police shooting raises civil liberties issues, and every use of deadly force is investigated to see whether it was justified.

During a 2015 investigation conducted after the highly publicized shooting death of Michael Brown in Ferguson, Missouri, the *Washington Post* found that in 74 percent of all fatal police shoot-

Very few police officers are ever involved in a shooting. A study found that 90 percent of these shootings involved suspects who had attacked or threatened others.

ings, the people who were killed had already fired shots, brandished a gun, or attacked a person with a weapon or their bare hands. "These 595 cases include fatal shootings that followed a wide range of violent crimes, including shootouts, stabbings, hostage situations, carjackings and assaults," stated the *Washington Post*. Another 16 percent of the shootings occurred "after incidents that did not involve firearms or active attacks but featured other potentially dangerous threats."[37] A total of 90 percent of the cases involved suspects who had attacked police officers or civilians or made direct threats. In such cases, investigations usually find that the use of deadly force is justified and does not violate the person's civil liberties.

When Deadly Force Becomes Controversial

The *Washington Post* researchers found that in about 5 percent of the cases, there was not enough information available to draw any conclusions, leaving 5 percent of the shootings that "occurred under the kind of circumstances that raise doubt and draw public outcry."[38] In those cases, the police said that the suspects failed to follow their orders, made sudden movements, or were shot accidentally. For example, in 2017 a pest control worker named Daniel Shaver was killed while receiving contradictory police orders. Shaver was seen by guests at a La Quinta Inn & Suites hotel in Mesa, Arizona, pointing a rifle out of a fifth-floor window. Police were summoned to the scene with the warning that the suspect was armed. They did not know that the weapon Shaver had was a pellet gun he sometimes used in his work.

The two officers, Sergeant Charles Langley and Officer Philip Brailsford, ordered Shaver and his companion to come out of the room and kneel on the floor. A video taken at the scene show that both people were unarmed. "Do not put your hands down for any reason," Langley commanded. "Your hands go back in the small of your back or down, we are going to shoot you, do you understand me?" Shaver, who was intoxicated and appeared to be in tears, assented. Langley then told Shaver, "Crawl towards me." Shaver lowered his hands to the floor and began moving toward the officers. After a few seconds, Shaver twisted to the right and reached toward his waistband. Langley shouted "Don't!"[39] and Brailsford shot Shaver five times with his AR-15 rifle. Shaver did not survive. Brailsford was charged with second-degree murder and a lesser manslaughter charge but was acquitted by a jury. "This video demonstrates how far we have gone as a country in accepting the culture of police violence," writes Jeffery Robinson, the ACLU's deputy legal director. "Policing in America has advanced to the state where anyone can be killed for no good reason."[40]

> "Policing in America has advanced to the state where anyone can be killed for no good reason."[40]
>
> —Deputy legal director Jeffery Robinson of the ACLU

Racial Disparities

Both Brailsford and Shaver were white, and whites make up 52 percent of the people killed by police. However, advocacy groups such as Black Lives Matter point out that African Americans make up a higher percentage of police shooting fatalities than their percentage of the overall population. This suggests that a disproportionate number of African Americans die in confrontations with police. A 2016 study conducted by James Buehler, a professor of health management and policy at Drexel University in Philadelphia, expands on this topic. Buehler's found that while more whites than blacks are killed by police, based on the relative numbers of each race in the general population, black men are nearly three times as likely as white men to be killed by police. Native Americans or Alaska Natives also are nearly three times as likely to be killed as whites, and Hispanic men are nearly twice as likely, the researchers found. "My study is a reminder that there are, indeed, substantial disparities in the rates of legal intervention deaths, and that ongoing attention to the underlying reasons for this disparity is warranted,"[41] said Buehler.

The reasons underlying the disparity are important in light of civil liberties. If the police are treating all races the same and responding only to the danger of a situation, then no one's civil liberties are being violated. However, if police officers treat members of one racial group worse than members of another, then that would be a violation of the Equal Protection Clause of the Fourteenth Amendment. This amendment states, among other things, that "no state shall . . . deny to any person within its jurisdiction the equal protection of the laws."

Buehler's study is not the only one to suggest that African Americans and Hispanics are shot a disproportional amount of the time. A 2017 study by VICE News, an online news and documentary company, conducted the first study that counted both fatal and nonfatal shootings by American police officers. The researchers studied shooting data from the police departments of forty-seven of the fifty largest cities in the country, home to 54 million people. The data set included information on 4,117 incidents and forty-four hundred subjects over seven years, from 2010 through 2016. Several police departments said they did not keep racial statistics or chose not to release them. As a result, race information was available for only about 68 percent of incidents. Like other studies, VICE News found that police killed 1,382 people over the seven-year period in these cities. This was in line with counts of the nation as a whole, which has a population six times greater than do the cities in the study. What surprised the researchers is that there were an additional 2,730 nonfatal shootings—about twice as many as the fatal shootings. Of these, 55 percent of the total involved African Americans. That is more than double the percentage of the black populations in the cities. When compared to the entire populations of the cities,

"My study is a reminder that there are, indeed, substantial disparities in the rates of legal intervention deaths, and that ongoing attention to the underlying reasons for this disparity is warranted."[41]

—James Buehler, a professor of health management and policy at Drexel University

Race Is the Most Important Factor in Police Shootings

Reporter Chantal Da Silva describes research showing racial disparities in fatal police shootings:

> Black people are three times more likely to be killed by police in the United States than white people, according to data from Mapping Police Violence. . . .
>
> Now researchers say they have been able to demonstrate a link between structural racism and racial disparities in fatal police shootings of unarmed victims in a groundbreaking study.
>
> Boston University School of Public Health (BUSPH) researchers say their findings show that states with a greater degree of structural racism tend to have higher racial disparities in fatal police shootings of unarmed victims. . . .
>
> Data from Mapping Police Violence shows that of 1,147 people killed by police in the U.S. in 2017, 25 percent, or 282 people, were black, despite making up only 13 percent of the population.
>
> The organization also found that 30 percent of black people killed by police in 2015 were unarmed, compared to 21 percent of white victims.
>
> While some have suggested that the high percentage of black people killed by police could be explained by greater interaction with officers, [BUSPH professor Michael] Siegel said that the BUSPH study controlled for rates [of] arrest and still found a strong association between the racial disparity in unarmed fatal police shootings and structural racism in states.

Chantal Da Silva, "US Police Shootings Reflect Structural Racism Across States, Study Finds," *Newsweek*, February 8, 2018. www.newsweek.com.

police shot black people two and a half times more often than white people. Police shot Hispanics slightly more often than whites, and Asians less often than any other race. Critics suggest this is clear evidence that blacks are being deprived of equal protection because they are more likely to be the victims of lethal force.

Other Factors in Police Shootings

Using general population figures as a measuring stick for racial disparities can be misleading, however, because it assumes that there are no other factors that might contribute to higher totals for some groups. For example, 50.8 percent of the total US population is

Race Is Not the Most Important Factor in Police Shootings

Author Nick Selby takes issue with reports that race is the major factor behind fatal police shootings:

> The media would have Americans believe that race is the single most important and predictive element of fatal encounters between police and civilians. . . . With a few notable exceptions, violent criminal attacks are the best predictor of whom police might shoot in America. . . .
>
> In 2015, two-thirds of unarmed people of any race killed by police had been in the process of committing violent crime or property destruction. Fourteen percent were engaged in domestic violence. Ten percent were committing a robbery, 20 percent a burglary or vandalism, and 21 percent an assault on another civilian. . . .
>
> Further, more than half of the unarmed people killed by police suffered from mental-health issues, drug intoxication, physical disability, or some combination of them. That's something public-health policies can address head-on. . . .
>
> Police are already conducting work to identify and re-train or fire the demonstrably small number of its ranks who behave inappropriately. To presume that solves society's ills is short-sighted. We must look to reasons other than simple racism on the part of the police, who end up holding the ball for a lot of failed systemic issues.

Nick Selby, "Police Aren't Targeting and Killing Black Men," *National Review*, July 17, 2017. www.nationalreview.com.

female, and 49.2 percent is male. Based on population only, one would expect about half of the police shooting deaths to involve women and about half to involve men. But in 2017, 95 percent of police shooting deaths involved men. This is because men are much more likely than women to be brandishing a gun or otherwise involved in situations that call for lethal force.

> "Deadly force has a disproportionate effect on nonwhite people, that's true, but nonwhite people disproportionately engage in behavior that is criminal and dangerous."[42]
>
> —Nick Selby, author and law enforcement officer

The same logic applies to race. Although people of every race commit crimes, crime rates are not the same among all the racial groups for a variety of social and economic reasons. For example, Asian Americans make up 4.8 percent of the US population but only 1.5 percent of the federal prison population. The Asian federal incarceration rate is disproportionately low. By contrast, Hispanics make up 9.1 percent of the US population but 33.8 percent of the federal prison population. The Hispanic federal incarceration rate is disproportionately high. Similarly, police shootings are less common among groups with lower crime rates than among groups with higher crime rates. "Deadly force has a disproportionate effect on nonwhite people, that's true, but nonwhite people disproportionately engage in behavior that is criminal and dangerous,"[42] writes author and law enforcement officer Nick Selby.

In January 2018, Roland Fryer, a professor of economics at Harvard University, published a study that looked past raw percentages of populations and instead factored in 125 different variables that could come into play during police use of force. These variables included the crimes that led to the encounters. For example, an armed robbery is more likely to lead to a shooting than an arrest for shoplifting. Fryer also analyzed the behavior of the person being arrested, including whether or not the suspect was armed, brandished a weapon, or even shot at the police. After factoring in all of the variables, Fryer found that blacks and Hispanics are still more than 50 percent more likely than whites to experience some form of force in interactions with police. The disproportionate use of force on blacks and Hispanics involved pushing, shoving, handcuffing, and baton and Taser use. However, it did not include fatal shootings. "In stark contrast to non-lethal uses of force, we find that, conditional on a police interaction, there are no racial differences in officer-involved shootings," wrote Fryer. In fact, Fryer found that African Americans are 23.5 percent less likely than whites to be shot by police in high-risk encounters. Hispanics are 8.5 percent less likely than whites to be shot in such situations. Fryer is not sure why this is. "Given the stream of video 'evidence,' which many take to be indicative of structural racism in police departments across America, the ensuing and understandable

A study found that blacks and Hispanics are 50 percent more likely than whites to experience some form of force in their interactions with police. However, the study also found that this was not the case for officer-involved fatal shootings.

outrage in black communities across America, and the results from our previous analysis of non-lethal uses of force, the results [on shootings] are startling,"[43] Fryer wrote. He speculated that knowing that every police shooting will be investigated, whereas other uses of force will not, might cause officers to set aside any racial biases they might have and focus only on the situation at hand when deploying deadly force.

The victimization of blacks in situations involving deadly force was addressed by Philadelphia police commissioner Charles Ramsey in 2015. Philadelphia police shot 394 suspects between 2007 and 2013. Blacks make up 42 percent of the city's population but were involved in 81 percent of the police shootings. When asked about that statistic at a press conference, Ramsey said, "Well, about 85 percent of our homicide victims are African American. About 85 percent of people who do the homicide are African American. So that's right in the ballpark." Ramsey, who is black, added, "Listen, in case you haven't noticed, I'm black myself so I'm not real proud of the fact that we have a disproportionate amount of crime occurring in African-American communities."[44] The Department of Justice (DOJ), which conducted a review of the shootings, made ninety-one recommendations to improve the Philadelphia police department, including more frequent and better training of the officers.

DOJ Reforms

Philadelphia was one of seven cities that the DOJ required to adopt reforms related to officer-involved shootings. According to a study of DOJ statistics by VICE News, police departments that were forced to take on reforms through binding agreements with the DOJ saw a 25 percent decline the first year after entering into the agreements. Cities that voluntarily adopted DOJ reforms saw a 32 percent decline in officer-involved shootings in the first year.

Although police shootings fell in the cities with federal oversight, homicide rates went up. A rise in violence in cities covered by the DOJ reforms, including Chicago, Baltimore, and St. Louis, drove a 10.8 percent increase in murders nationwide, according to data from the FBI. As a result, US attorney general Jeff Sessions announced in 2017 that the DOJ would review all such oversight agreements. "It is a basic civil right to be safe in your home and your neighborhood," Sessions said during a speech before the National Association of Attorneys General. "Rather than dictating to local police how to do their jobs—or spending scarce federal resources to sue them in court—we should use our money, research and expertise to help them figure out what is happening and determine the best ways to fight crime."[45] Ron Davis, who headed the DOJ's Office of Community Oriented Policing Services, which oversaw the DOJ reforms, says that Sessions's approach is misguided. "I think it's dangerous,"[46] Davis says. It remains to be seen whether changes in the DOJ approach will lead to more police shootings and more equal protection violations or if they will reduce crime without diminishing civil liberties.

CHAPTER 4

Discrimination

Throughout American history, the police have often been accused of treating members of racial or ethnic groups differently and worse than they treat white people. For example, a 1929 report by the Illinois Association for Criminal Justice found that although African Americans made up just 5 percent of the area's population, they made up 30 percent of the victims of police killings. "There was a lot of one-on-one conflict between police and citizens and a lot of it was initiated by the police,"[47] says Malcolm D. Holmes, a sociology professor at the University of Wyoming. Such discrimination is a violation of people's civil liberties under the Equal Protection Clause of the Fourteenth Amendment.

Profiling

Many social critics claim that police routinely single out a person for surveillance, a traffic stop, or a stop-and-frisk encounter on the basis of that individual's age, race, ethnicity, or sexual orientation. This practice is known as profiling. When it involves race, it is known as racial profiling. "For many of us, the sight of a police officer is comforting. Someone's there to keep the order, intervene in an emergency, catch the bad guys. But for millions of other Americans, seeing a uniformed officer is reason for a slight uneasiness or even outright fear. Those are the folks who have been or think they will be stopped simply because of the color of their skin,"[48] said reporter Rita Bralver in a CBS *Sunday Morning* segment titled, "Driving While Black or Brown." The title of the segment came from a nickname that minorities give to the treatment they sometimes receive from the police. "Black people are stopped for no reason," Sheryl Crayton, a school administrator in Los Angeles, told Bralver. "I didn't think it would happen to me because I'm a mature African American, you know."[49]

Since a person's race, ethnicity, or dress is not grounds for reasonable suspicion, such treatment is a violation of the person's civil liberties. A spokesperson for the Los Angeles Police Department denied the charge of racial profiling. "When you look at our law enforcement efforts, they're clearly color blind,"[50] said Commander David Kalish.

Racial profiling played a big part in the 2012 class action lawsuit against the City of New York for its stop-and-frisk program. According to *Forbes*, 92 percent of all NYPD stop-and-frisk episodes in 2012 involved minorities. The unequal application of the stop-and-frisk procedure led the Center for Constitutional Rights to allege that the NYPD violated not only the Fourth Amendment protection against unreasonable searches but also the Fourteenth Amendment's Equal Protection Clause. "The named plaintiffs in the case—David Floyd, David Ourlicht, Lalit Clarkson, and Deon Dennis—represent the thousands of primarily Black and Latino New Yorkers who have been stopped without any cause on the way to work or home from school, in front of their house, or just walking down the street,"[51] stated the Center for Constitutional Rights.

"Targeting young black and Hispanic men for stops based on the alleged criminal conduct of other young black or Hispanic men violates the bedrock principles of equality."[52]

—US district judge Shira Scheindlin

The racial profiling aspect of the lawsuit was one of the major reasons why district judge Shira Scheindlin ruled in favor of the plaintiffs and against the NYPD. "No one should live in fear of being stopped whenever he leaves his home to go about the activities of daily life," wrote Scheindlin. "Targeting young black and Hispanic men for stops based on the alleged criminal conduct of

Protesters in New York City march in opposition to the city's controversial stop-and-frisk program. According to one study, 92 percent of all NYPD stops involved minorities.

other young black or Hispanic men violates the bedrock principles of equality."[52] Scheindlin also criticized city officials for overseeing the stop-and-frisk program. Mayor Michael Bloomberg strongly defended the program, saying that it helped bring street crime down. "The City's highest officials have turned a blind eye to the evidence that officers are conducting stops in a racially discriminatory manner," wrote Scheindlin. "In their zeal to defend a policy that they believe to be effective, they have willfully ignored overwhelming proof that the policy of singling out 'the right people' is racially discriminatory and therefore violates the United States Constitution."[53]

> "It's one thing to be arrested. What's worse is to be arrested and deprived of your liberties because you're gay."[54]
>
> —Attorney Bruce Nickerson

Targeting Gay Men

Sometimes people are targeted not for their race or ethnic background but because of their sexual orientation. In November 2017, noted gay rights attorney Bruce Nickerson filed a lawsuit against the San Jose Police Department in California for targeting gay men for arrest. According to the lawsuit, undercover police officers posing as gay men suggested sex acts to men in public places and arrested men who reciprocated interest. The cases against six men arrested by the police decoys were dismissed by Santa Clara County Superior Court judge Jose S. Franco, who ruled in 2016 that targeting gay men while ignoring similar conduct by heterosexuals was discriminatory. Nickerson asked for $1 million in damages for the violations of civil liberties. "It's one thing to be arrested," said Nickerson. "What's worse is to be arrested and deprived of your liberties because you're gay."[54]

Religious Profiling

In the aftermath of the September 11, 2001, terrorist attacks on the World Trade Center and the Pentagon, police also began to profile people on the basis of their religion. Since the nineteen 9/11 hijackers were Muslims and belonged to an Islamist extremist group, the NYPD began to monitor activities in mosques in an attempt to uncover potential terrorist plots. Informants known as mosque crawlers infiltrated mosques in largely Muslim communities and spied on their activities. In 2016 the NYPD settled a federal lawsuit brought by eight Muslims alleging the department had violated their civil liberties by targeting them because of their religion. "The NYPD program is founded upon a false and constitutionally impermissible premise: that Muslim religious identity is a legitimate criterion for selection of law-enforcement surveillance targets,"[55] stated the lawsuit, which was brought by Muslim Advocates, a California-based civil rights group. "The American Muslim community was victimized by the New York Police Department and their warrant-less surveillance,"[56] said Syed Farhaj

Michael Bennett Was Racially Profiled

On September 6, 2017, star football player Michael Bennett of the Seattle Seahawks posted an open letter on Twitter, alleging that he was racially profiled by the Las Vegas Metropolitan Police.

On Saturday, August 26, 2017, I was in Las Vegas to attend the Mayweather-McGregor fight on my day off. After the fight while heading back to my hotel several hundred people heard what sounded like gun shots. Like many of the people in the area I ran away from the sound, looking for safety. Las Vegas police officers singled me out and pointed their guns at me for doing nothing more than simply being a black man in the wrong place at the wrong time.

A police officer ordered me to get on the ground. As I laid on the ground, complying with his commands to not move, he placed his gun near my head and warned me that if I moved he would "blow my . . . head off.". . .

The Officers' excessive use of force was unbearable. I felt helpless as I lay there on the ground handcuffed facing the real-life threat of being killed. All I could think of was "I'm going to die for no other reason than I am black and my skin color is somehow a threat."

Quoted in Chuck Schilken, "Seahawks' Michael Bennett Claims Police Used Excessive Force Against Him for 'Being a Black Man,'" *Los Angeles Times*, September 7, 2017. www.latimes.com.

Hassan, one of the plaintiffs. An army reservist who served in the Iraq War, Hassan said he stopped attending one mosque after he learned that it was under surveillance, according to NYPD files.

As part of the settlement, the NYPD did not admit to any wrongdoing, but it agreed to strengthen safeguards against illegal surveillance of Muslims in terrorism investigations. Among the changes, the NYPD placed a civilian representative on a com-

Michael Bennett Was Not Racially Profiled

Las Vegas Metropolitan Police undersheriff Kevin McMahill briefed reporters on the Michael Bennett incident. In this excerpt, McMahill states that he sees no evidence of racial profiling:

> One of the teams that cleared the casino then exited the casino at the door to regroup and were redirected back toward the Drai's Nightclub inside of the casino. As they moved toward the nightclub, an individual later identified as Bennett was seen crouched down behind a gaming machine as the officers approached. Once Bennett was in the officer's view he quickly ran out of the south doors, jumped over a wall onto Flamingo Road, east of Las Vegas Boulevard, into traffic. Due to Bennett's actions and the information officers had at the time, they believed Bennett may have been involved in the shooting and they gave chase. Bennett was placed in handcuffs and detained while officers determined whether or not he was involved in the original incident. . . .
>
> Many of the folks today have called this an incident of bias-based policing—police officers focused solely on the race of an individual that they are going to stop. I can tell you as I stand here today I see no evidence of that. I see no evidence that race played any role in this incident.

Las Vegas Metropolitan Police, "Undersheriff Kevin McMahill Briefs the Media on Incident Involving Michael Bennett," YouTube, September 6, 2017. www.youtube.com.

mittee that meets monthly to review the investigations. The committee has the authority to report any civil rights concerns to the mayor or the court. "We are committed to strengthening the relationship between our administration and communities of faith so that residents of every background feel respected and protected,"[57] said New York mayor Bill de Blasio. The NYPD demographics unit that conducted the surveillance was shut down in 2014.

Selective Enforcement

Sometimes profiling can extend to certain areas of a city and to the races or ethnicities of the people living there. When police concentrate their efforts on certain areas, it is known as selective enforcement. Like other profiling, selective enforcement can violate a person's civil liberties under the Equal Protection Clause. For example, a 2016 report prepared by Columbia Law School professor Jeffrey Fagan found evidence that federal agents with the ATF targeted minorities for drug stings in Chicago. Fully 91 percent of the 94 people arrested in the sting operations since 2006 were either black or Hispanic. Fagan found only a 0.1 percent probability that such a high percentage of minorities could have been selected by chance, even if the agents followed ATF guidelines and only targeted people with criminal records that suggested they might be likely to participate in the suggested crimes. According to the findings, Fagan wrote, "the ATF is discriminating on the basis of race."[58]

On the basis of the report and other evidence, the Federal Criminal Justice Clinic (FCJC) has filed motions to dismiss ten federal criminal cases involving forty defendants due to racially selective law enforcement that violated the Equal Protection Clause of the Fourteenth Amendment. The FCJC, a program of the University of Chicago Law School, represents indigent defendants charged with federal crimes. The organization contends that the ATF "unconstitutionally discriminated on the basis of race in targeting almost exclusively people of color . . . in violation of Equal Protection principles."[59] In March 2018, admitting no wrongdoing, federal prosecutors offered plea deals to forty-three men charged in the ATF stings. The offers included no minimum sentences, greatly reducing the possible prison time for the defendants.

Singling Out Chinese Businesses

Blacks and Hispanics are not the only races singled out for selective enforcement. Police in Philadelphia have been accused of targeting ethnic Chinese business owners in the selective enforcement of a law that requires businesses on residential blocks to close by 11 p.m. According to a report compiled by Philadelphia city councilman David Oh, more than 90 percent of the businesses fined under the ordinance in 2015 and 2016 were Chinese takeout restaurants but nearby delis, pizzerias, and fried chicken restaurants had not been cited. The study "raises important questions, including the possibility of race-based enforcement,"[60] the city attorney admitted in a statement. Selective enforcement on the basis of race or ethnicity is also forbidden by the Equal Protection Clause.

> "The officer says, 'My job is to write tickets. I don't care if you go to court. I'll keep coming till you close.'"[61]
>
> —Mei Ying Luo, restaurant owner

Grace House, a Chinese takeout restaurant owned by Mei Ying Luo and her husband, is one of the restaurants that was a victim of selective enforcement by Philadelphia police. Luo has received dozens of tickets for violating the curfew. Luo even received a municipal court ruling saying that her restaurant was open legally because the block on which it is located is 20 percent commercial, making it exempt from the curfew. Luo informed the raiding police officers of the court's finding, but they continued to cite her. "The officer says, 'My job is to write tickets. I don't care if you go to court. I'll keep coming till you close,'" Luo told the *Philadelphia Inquirer* newspaper. "I say, 'I'm not the bad guy! We are a service to the neighborhood!'"[61] Another business owner, Ling Lin, closed her Good Luck Restaurant after receiving multiple citations and having the police order her customers away, even though a judge had ruled her restaurant was open legally as well. In all, twenty-seven Chinese takeout restaurants were hit with curfew violations between 2015 and 2017.

Under pressure from Councilman Oh, the deputy commissioners of the Philadelphia Police Department suspended enforcement of the curfew ordinance in October 2017. "It is certainly not our intent to apply any type of law enforcement in a discriminatory manner," said Philadelphia police captain Sekou Kinebrew.

"In fact to that end a couple of weeks back one of our deputy commissioners sent down an order suspending that particular ordinance to close at 11pm while we look at it."[62]

The selective enforcement of the Philadelphia restaurant curfew is reminiscent of the first Supreme Court ruling that found selective enforcement on the basis of race or ethnicity to be a violation of constitutional rights. On August 4, 1885, a Chinese national named Yick Wo in San Francisco was cited under an 1880 law prohibiting the operation of a laundry in a wooden building without a special permit. Although he had operated his laundry for twenty-two years in compliance with all other health and safety regulations, Wo was cited and found guilty. Wo and another Chinese national challenged their convictions, charging that they and more than 150 other Chinese nationals had been arrested for not having the special permit while eighty laundries with non-Chinese owners were allowed to operate without the

Hundreds of people walk on a street in San Francisco's famed Chinatown. In the 1880s, Chinatown was involved in one of the first Supreme Court rulings to find that selective police enforcement is a violation of rights.

same permit. The California Supreme Court and the US Circuit Court of Appeals upheld their convictions, but the US Supreme Court overturned them, stating,

> The fact of this discrimination is admitted [by the sheriff of San Francisco]. No reason for it is shown, and the conclusion cannot be resisted that no reason for it exists except hostility to the race and nationality to which the petitioners belong, and which, in the eye of the law, is not justified. The discrimination is, therefore, illegal, and the public administration which enforces it is a denial of the equal protection of the laws and a violation of the Fourteenth Amendment of the Constitution. The imprisonment of the petitioners is, therefore, illegal, and they must be discharged.[63]

This ruling showed that although a law may be constitutional as it is written, its selective enforcement by the police can violate the Constitution. The ruling in the Wo case has been cited in more than 150 other Supreme Court cases dealing with discrimination.

Focusing on Neighborhoods

Selective enforcement can apply to entire neighborhoods, not just individuals. In the Wo case, for example, San Francisco police focused on an area of the city known as Chinatown—named for its high population of Chinese immigrants—when enforcing its permit law. Jeffrey Fagan, one of the researchers who conducted the study on the ATF sting operation, also studied police procedures in the NYPD stop-and-frisk program from 2004 to 2011. He found that the NYPD regularly conducted so-called vertical patrols in multistory public housing buildings, making tens of thousands of Terry stops each year. Fagan found that during these patrols, both uniformed and undercover officers stopped and questioned residents and visitors with little suspicion of wrongdoing, "usually alleging trespass to justify the stop."

Fagan found that the incidence rate for trespass stops and arrests was more than two times greater in public housing than in the surrounding neighborhoods. The percentage of blacks and Hispanics living in the public housing was also higher than in the surrounding areas. "The pattern of racially selective enforcement suggests the potential for systemic violations of the Fourteenth Amendment's prohibition on racial discrimination,"[64] Fagan wrote. His report was included as evidence in the stop-and-frisk lawsuit presented to Judge Sheindlin.

Police sometimes target higher-income neighborhoods for enforcement, especially when the area is changing from a low-income area to a high-income area—a process known as gentrification. Many older neighborhoods in big cities undergo a change as buildings are refurbished and rented or sold to young working professionals. New businesses appealing to the upscale residents move in, and longtime residents and businesses are displaced. During the transition, the new residents may call the police with complaints about minor criminal activities that were not reported before, such as loitering and noise violations, resulting in a greater police presence. "As demographics shift, activity that was previously considered normal becomes suspicious, and newcomers—many of whom are white—are more inclined to get law enforcement involved,"[65] writes Abdallah Fayyad, a reporter for the *Atlantic*.

Longtime residents sometimes refer to this kind of selective enforcement as the criminalization of their neighborhood. "In a number of cities, people have observed that enforcement of low-level offenses against black and brown people increases when neighborhoods are prime for gentrification," says Paul Butler, a former federal prosecutor in Washington, DC. "The concern when there are misdemeanor offenses is that neighborhoods seem unsafe or disorderly and that decreases their attractiveness for gentrification."[66] Regardless of the reasoning, selective enforcement on the basis of race is a violation of the Equal Protection Clause of the Constitution.

Underenforcement

Most people use the phrase *selective enforcement* to describe high levels of enforcement targeting racial or ethnic groups. However, the phrase can also be used describe too little enforcement. "The principal injury suffered by African-Americans in relation to criminal matters is not overenforcement but underenforcement of the laws,"[67] wrote Randall Kennedy, a law professor at Harvard University, in his influential 1997 book, *Race, Crime, and the Law*. Kennedy, who is African American, called for greater police protection in black neighborhoods.

Alexandra Natapoff, a professor of law at the University of California, Irvine, agrees. In an article in the *Fordham Law Review* entitled "Underforcement," Natapoff writes, "Within certain communities or institutions—what I will call 'underenforcement zones'—the state routinely and predictably fails to enforce the law to the detriment of vulnerable residents." In this situation, the police do not arrest people for certain crimes, such as prostitution, selling drugs, and violations of nuisance laws, such as drinking in public. People soon realize their crimes will likely go unpunished, leading to greater criminal activity and less-safe neighborhoods. Some people wonder how underenforcement and overenforcement can be occurring at the same time, but Natapoff sees the two as linked. She writes, "Over- and underenforcement are twin symptoms of a deeper democratic weakness of the criminal system: its non-responsiveness to the needs of the poor, racial minorities, and the otherwise politically vulnerable."[68]

Police have also underenforced crimes in which women are the victims, especially rape. "In underenforced arenas, the criminal justice system withholds its protective resources from groups deemed unworthy of protection," writes Deborah Tuerkheimer, a professor of law at Northwestern University. "Unremedied injuries suffered by women, in particular, have historically been the norm, just as gender bias has long been an intractable feature of our criminal justice landscape."[69] Historically, police have not taken rape allegations as seriously as they have other crimes. This is a form of discrimination against the victims and a violation of the Equal Protection Clause. As a result of this underenforcement, many women do not report being victims of the crime. According to a 2017 study by the DOJ, 77 percent of rape and sexual assault victims do not report the crime to police. A 2013 DOJ study found that a fifth of nonstudent rape victims ages eighteen to twenty-four who did not report the crime said it was because the "police would not or could not do anything to help."[70]

A study of the DOJ's National Crime Victimization Survey, conducted by the Rape, Abuse, and Incest National Network, found that only 9 percent of rapists are prosecuted, only 5 percent lead to a felony conviction, and only 3 percent of rapists ever spend time in prison. When the DOJ received allegations that the Missoula Police Department (MPD) in Montana was mishandling

Police have underinvestigated crimes in which women are the victims, especially rape. Historically, police have not taken rape allegations as seriously as they have other crimes.

rape cases, it launched an investigation into the underenforcement of rape law in the city. A year later, the DOJ issued a report finding that "deficiencies in MPD's response to sexual assault compromise the effectiveness of sexual assault investigations from the outset, make it more difficult to uncover the truth, and have the effect of depriving female sexual assault victims of basic legal protections."[71] The MPD's underenforcement was a violation of the victim's civil liberties, according to Tuerkheimer. She writes, "The Justice Department concluded that MPD's failed response to sexual assault violated the Equal Protection Clause."[72]

> "The Justice Department concluded that [the Missoula Police Department]'s failed response to sexual assault violated the Equal Protection Clause."[72]
>
> —Deborah Tuerkheimer, a professor of law at Northwestern University

Under a settlement with the DOJ, the MPD agreed to improve its response to sexual assault, including by combating gender bias. The MDP was required to include the International Association of Chiefs of Police model policy on investigating sexual assault into its training. By 2015, more rape victims were reporting the crime to police and choosing to pursue their complaints. On May 11, 2015, the DOJ announced that the MPD had fully complied with the agreement. In addition, the DOJ has stated that police departments have a legal obligation to eliminate gender bias in the enforcement of the law. "The Justice Department's most recent intervention is promising," writes Tuerkheimer. "This much was made incontestable: the underenforcement of rape law is a problem of constitutional dimension; unequal protection is a federal concern."[73]

Introduction: The Paradox of Police Power

1. Quoted in USHistory.org, "The Declaration of Independence." www.ushistory.org.
2. John Locke, "Second Treatise, 1689," in *The Founders Constitution*, ed. by Philip B. Kurland and Ralph Lerner. http://press-pubs.uchicago.edu.
3. Quoted in USHistory.org, "The Declaration of Independence."
4. Quoted in Justia, "Dennis et al. v. United States, 341 U.S. 494 (1951)." https://supreme.justia.com.

Chapter 1: Investigative Procedures

5. Center for Constitutional Rights, "Improved NYPD Stop-and-Frisk Training Not a Silver Bullet, Say Rights Attorneys," November 16, 2017. https://ccrjustice.org.
6. Quoted in R. Robin McDonald, "Suspended Sheriff to Pay $3M After Warrantless Search of High School Students," *Daily Report*, November 14, 2017. www.law.com.
7. US Supreme Court, "Opinions of the Court—2012: Florida v. Jardines." www.supremecourt.gov.
8. Quoted in Justia, "Kyllo v. United States, 533 U.S. 27 (2001)." https://supreme.justia.com.
9. Quoted in Justia, "United States v. Jones, 565 U.S. 400 (2012)." https://supreme.justia.com.
10. Quoted in Justia, "Katz v. United States, 389 U.S. 347 (1967)." https://supreme.justia.com.
11. Quoted in Justia, "Smith v. Maryland, 442 U.S. 735 (1979)." https://supreme.justia.com.
12. Quoted in Justia, "United States v. Miller, 425 U.S. 435 (1976)." https://supreme.justia.com.
13. US Supreme Court, "Oral Arguments: Timothy Ivory Carpenter v. United States," November 29, 2017. www.supremecourt.gov.

14. US Supreme Court, "Oral Arguments: Timothy Ivory Carpenter v. United States."

Chapter 2: Interrogation Techniques

15. Quoted in Justia, "Ashcraft v. Tennessee, 322 U.S. 143 (1944)." https://supreme.justia.com.
16. Quoted in Justia, "Harris v. United States, 331 U.S. 145 (1947)." https://supreme.justia.com.
17. US Supreme Court, "Opinions of the Court—2013: Riley v. California." www.supremecourt.gov.
18. US Supreme Court, "Opinions of the Court—2013: Riley v. California."
19. Quoted in Joshua Dressler, Alan C. Michaels, and Ric Simmons, *Understanding Criminal Procedure*, vol. 1, *Investigation*. Durham, NC: Carolina Academic, 2017, p. 389.
20. Quoted in John Wilkens and Mark Sauer, "Haunting Questions: The Stephanie Crowe Murder Case," SignOnSanDiego.com, May 12, 1999. http://legacy.sandiegouniontribune.com.
21. National Registry of Exonerations, "Guilty Pleas and False Confessions," November 24, 2015. www.law.umich.edu.
22. Quoted in Legal Information Institute, "Miranda v. Arizona," Cornell Law School. www.law.cornell.edu.
23. Quoted in Alan M. Schutzman, "Rhode Island v. Innis," *Hofstra Law Review*, vol. 9, no. 2, 1981. http://scholarlycommons.law.hofstra.edu.
24. Quoted in Schutzman, "Rhode Island v. Innis."
25. Quoted in Schutzman, "Rhode Island v. Innis."
26. Quoted in Schutzman, "Rhode Island v. Innis."
27. Quoted in Justia, "Rhode Island v. Innis, 446 U.S. 291 (1980)." https://supreme.justia.com.
28. Quoted in Justia, "Rhode Island v. Innis, 446 U.S. 291 (1980)."
29. Quoted in Justia, "Salinas v. Texas, 570 U.S. ___ (2013)." https://supreme.justia.com.
30. Quoted in Justia, "Salinas v. Texas, 570 U.S. ___ (2013)."
31. Quoted in Legal Information Institute, "Miranda v. Arizona."
32. Alexander Abad-Santos, "The Supreme Court Decided Your Silence Can Be Used Against You," *Atlantic*, June 17, 2013. www.theatlantic.com.

33. Quoted in Spencer Sherman, "Court Makes Exception to Miranda Rule," *United Press International*, June 12, 1984. www.upi.com.

Chapter 3: The Use of Force

34. Quoted in Nathan O'Neal and Marvin Clemons, "ACLU Wants Choke-Hold Practices to End After Man's Police Custody Death at Venetian," *3News Las Vegas*, May 15, 2017. http://news3lv.com.

35. Quoted in American Civil Liberties Union, "ACLU of Nevada Welcomes Updated LVMPD Chokehold Policy," September 21, 2017. www.aclu.org.

36. Quoted in Rob Arthur et al., "Shot by Cops and Forgotten," *VICE News*, December 11, 2017. https://news.vice.com.

37. Amy Brittain, "On Duty, Under Fire," *Washington Post*, October 24, 2015. www.washingtonpost.com.

38. Brittain, "On Duty, Under Fire."

39. Quoted in Jeffery Robinson, "'You're Fucked': The Acquittal of Officer Brailsford and the Crisis of Police Impunity," *Speak Freely* (blog), American Civil Liberties Union, December 12, 2017. www.aclu.org.

40. Robinson, "'You're Fucked.'"

41. Quoted in Jacqueline Howard, "Black Men Nearly 3 Times as Likely to Die from Police Use of Force, Study Says," CNN, December 20, 2016. https://edition.cnn.com.

42. Quoted in Arthur et al., "Shot by Cops and Forgotten."

43. Roland G. Fryer Jr., "An Empirical Analysis of Racial Differences in Police Use of Force," National Bureau of Economic Research Working Paper, January 2018. www.nber.org.

44. Quoted in Jeff Brady, "Philadelphia Police Must Change Tactics, Justice Department Says," NPR, March 23, 2015. www.npr.org.

45. Jeff Sessions, "Attorney General Jeff Sessions Delivers Remarks at National Association of Attorneys General Annual Winter Meeting," US Department of Justice, February 28, 2017. www.justice.gov.

46. Quoted in Arthur et al., "Shot by Cops and Forgotten."

Chapter 4: Discrimination

47. Quoted in Katie Nodjimbadem, "The Long, Painful History of Police Brutality in the US," *Smithsonian*, July 27, 2017. www.smithsonianmag.com.

48. Quoted in CBSNews.com Staff, "Driving While Black or Brown," *Sunday Morning*, February 11, 2000. www.cbsnews.com.

49. Quoted in CBSNews.com Staff, "Driving While Black or Brown."

50. Quoted in CBSNews.com Staff, "Driving While Black or Brown."

51. Center for Constitutional Rights, "Floyd, et al. v. City of New York, et al.," December 13, 2017. https://ccrjustice.org.

52. Floyd v. City of New York, 959 F. Supp. 2d 540 (S.D. New York 2013). https://scholar.google.com.ph/scholar_case?case=3900561993131 97546&hl=en&as_sdt=2006&as_vis=1.

53. Quoted in Editorial Board, "Racial Discrimination in Stop-and-Frisk," *New York Times,* August 12, 2013. www.nytimes.com.

54. Quoted in Robert Salonga, "San Jose: Lawsuit Filed Against Police over Undercover Gay Sex Stings," *San Jose (CA) Mercury News*, November 16, 2017. www.mercurynews.com.

55. Quoted in Eileen Sullivan, "Muslims Sue to Stop NYPD Surveillance," NBC News, June 6, 2012. www.nbcnews.com.

56. Quoted in CBS/AP, "NYC Settles Lawsuits over Muslim Surveillance by Police," CBS News, January 7, 2016. www.cbsnews.com.

57. Quoted in CBS/AP, "NYC Settles Lawsuits over Muslim Surveillance by Police."

58. Quoted in Brad Heath, "ATF Drug Stings Targeted Minorities, Report Finds," *USA Today*, September 23, 2016. www.usatoday.com.

59. Alison Siegler and Judith P. Miller, "Federal Criminal Justice Clinic Moves to Dismiss Cases Because ATF Discriminated on the Basis of Race," University of Chicago Law School, September 24, 2016. www.law.uchicago.edu.

60. Quoted in Joseph N. DiStefano, "Selective Enforcement in Philly? Late-Night Pizza Shops OK; Chinese Takeouts Fined," *Philadelphia Inquirer*, October 16, 2017. www.philly.com.

61. Quoted in DiStefano, "Selective Enforcement in Philly?"
62. Quoted in Alicia Nieves, "Philly Councilman Working to Revamp Ordinance Allegedly Targeting Chinese Restaurants," Philly CBS, October 24, 2017. http://philadelphia.cbslocal.com.
63. Quoted in Justia, "Yick Wo v. Hopkins, 118 U.S. 356 (1886)." https://supreme.justia.com.
64. Jeffrey Fagan, Garth Davies, and Adam Carlis, "Race and Selective Enforcement in Public Housing," *Journal of Empirical Legal Studies*, vol. 9, no. 4, December 2012. http://online library.wiley.com.
65. Abdallah Fayyad, "The Criminalization of Gentrifying Neighborhoods," *Atlantic*, December 20, 2017. www.theatlantic.com.
66. Quoted in Fayyad, "The Criminalization of Gentrifying Neighborhoods."
67. Quoted in Craig Lambert, "Black, White, and Many Shades of Gray," *Harvard Magazine*, May/June 2013. https://harvard magazine.com.
68. Alexandra Natapoff, "Underforcement," *Fordham Law Review*, vol. 75, no. 3, 2006. https://ir.lawnet.fordham.edu.
69. Deborah Tuerkheimer, "Underenforcement as Unequal Protection," *Boston College Law Review*, vol. 57, no. 4, September 28, 2016. http://lawdigitalcommons.bc.edu.
70. Quoted in Tuerkheimer, "Underenforcement as Unequal Protection."
71. Quoted in Tuerkheimer, "Underenforcement as Unequal Protection."
72. Tuerkheimer, "Underenforcement as Unequal Protection."
73. Tuerkheimer, "Underenforcement as Unequal Protection."

Alliance for Justice

11 Dupont Circle NW, Suite 500
Washington, DC 20036
www.afj.org

The Alliance for Justice is a national association of more than 120 organizations. It advocates for the federal judiciary to protect constitutional values and human rights and to administer equal justice to all Americans.

American Civil Liberties Union (ACLU)

125 Broad St., Eighteenth Floor
New York, NY 10004
www.aclu.org

Established in 1920, the ACLU is a nonpartisan, nonprofit organization with more than 2 million members, activists, and supporters. The organization works in courts, legislatures, and communities to defend individual rights and liberties guaranteed under the Constitution and other laws of the United States.

Cato Institute

1000 Massachusetts Ave. NW
Washington, DC 20001
www.cato.org

The Cato Institute is a public policy research organization—a think tank—dedicated to the principles of individual liberty, limited government, free markets, and peace. Its scholars and analysts conduct independent, nonpartisan research on a wide range of policy issues, including criminal justice.

Center for Constitutional Rights (CCR)

666 Broadway, Seventh Floor
New York, NY 10012
https://ccrjustice.org

The CCR is dedicated to advancing and protecting the rights guaranteed by the US Constitution and the UN Universal Declaration of Human Rights. The center is committed to the creative use of law as a positive force for social change. It uses litigation, advocacy, and strategic communications to address a broad range of civil and human rights issues.

Fraternal Order of Police

701 Marriott Dr.
Nashville, TN 37214
www.fop.net

The Fraternal Order of Police is the world's largest organization of sworn law enforcement officers, with more than 330,000 members. It is committed to improving the working conditions of law enforcement officers and the safety of those they serve through education, legislation, information, community involvement, and employee representation.

International Association of Chiefs of Police (IACP)

44 Canal Center Plaza, Suite 200
Alexandria, VA 22314
www.theiacp.org

The IACP is a professional association for law enforcement worldwide. The IACP actively supports law enforcement through advocacy, outreach, education, and other programs. By engaging in strategic partnerships across the public safety spectrum, the IACP provides members with resources and support in all aspects of law enforcement policy and operations.

NAACP Legal Defense and Educational Fund (LDF)

40 Rector St., Fifth Floor
New York, NY 10006
www.naacpldf.org

The LDF is America's first—and still a leading—civil and human rights law firm. Through litigation, advocacy, and public education, the LDF seeks structural changes to expand democracy, eliminate disparities, and achieve racial justice in a society that fulfills the promise of equality for all Americans.

National Lawyers Guild
132 Nassau St., Suite 922
New York, NY 10038
www.nlg.org

The National Lawyers Guild is a progressive bar association dedi-cated to using law for the people. It includes lawyers, law stu-dents, and other legal professionals to work for social change at the local, regional, national, and international levels.

FOR FURTHER RESEARCH

Books

Laura Coates, *You Have the Right: A Constitutional Guide to Policing the Police*. New York: Karen Hunter, 2015.

James Duane, *You Have the Right to Remain Innocent*. New York: Little A, 2016.

William Dudley, *Do Police Abuse Their Powers?* San Diego, CA: ReferencePoint, 2017.

James Forman Jr., *Locking Up Our Own: Crime and Punishment in Black America*. New York: Farrar, Straus, and Giroux, 2017.

Barry Friedman, *Unwarranted: Policing Without Permission*. New York: Farrar, Straus, and Giroux, 2017.

Matthew Horace and Ron Harris, *The Black and the Blue: A Cop Reveals the Crimes, Racism, and Injustice in America's Law Enforcement*. New York: Hachette, 2018.

Andrea C. Nakaya, *Thinking Critically: Police Powers*. San Diego, CA: ReferencePoint, 2018.

Nick Selby, *In Context: Understanding Police Killings of Unarmed Civilians*. St. Augustine, FL: CIAI, 2016.

Internet Sources

Amy Brittain, "On Duty, Under Fire," *Washington Post*, October 24, 2015. www.washingtonpost.com/sf/investigative/2015/10/24/on-duty-under-fire/?tid=a_inl&utm_term=.091eba062f77.

Center for Constitutional Rights, "NYPD Stop-and-Frisk Statistics: 2009 and 2010," 2012. http://webarchive.loc.gov

/all/20120328093238/http://ccrjustice.org/files/CCR_Stop_and
_Frisk_Fact_Sheet.pdf.

Joseph Cohen, "Police Officer Wins Settlement from City That Fired Him for Not Shooting a Black Man," *Speak Freely* (blog), ACLU, February 12, 2018. www.aclu.org/blog/criminal-law-reform /reforming-police-practices/police-officer-wins-settlement-city -fired-him.

Abdallah Fayyad, "The Criminalization of Gentrifying Neighbor-hoods," *Atlantic*, December 20, 2017. www.theatlantic.com /politics/archive/2017/12/the-criminalization-of-gentrifying -neighborhoods/548837/.

Jeffery Robinson, "'You're Fucked': The Acquittal of Officer Brailsford and the Crisis of Police Impunity," *Speak Freely* (blog), ACLU, December 12, 2017. www.aclu.org/blog/criminal-law -reform/reforming-police-practices/youre-fucked-acquittal -officer-brailsford-and.

Nick Selby, "Guest Post: The 'Low-Hanging Fruit' of Police Re-form," *Washington Post*, June 20, 2016. www.washingtonpost .com/news/the-watch/wp/2016/06/20/guest-post-the-low -hanging-fruit-of-police-reform/?utm_term=.8dea6a5734d5.

John Sullivan et al., "Number of Fatal Shootings by Police Is Near-ly Identical to Last Year," *Washington Post*, July 1, 2017. www .washingtonpost.com/investigations/number-of-fatal-shootings -by-police-is-nearly-identical-to-last-year/2017/07/01/98726 cc6-5b5f-11e7-9fc6-c7ef4bc58d13_story.html?utm_term =.3b1a5b56c5a7.

Meredith Walker, as told to Alysia Santo, "A Black Mother's Sur-vival Guide for Her Teenage Son," Marshall Project, February 15, 2018. www.themarshallproject.org/2018/02/15/a-black-mother -s-survival-guide-for-her-teenage-son.

PICTURE CREDITS